50 FAVORITE FURNISHINGS BY
FRANK LLOYD WRIGHT

50 FAVORITE FURNISHINGS BY
FRANK LLOYD WRIGHT

DIANE MADDEX

SMITHMARK

This edition published 1999 by SMITHMARK Publishers, a division of U.S. Media Holdings, Inc., 115 West 18th Street, New York, NY 10011.

SMITHMARK books are available for bulk purchase for sales promotion and premium use. For details write or call the manager of special sales, SMITHMARK Publishers, 115 West 18th Street, New York, NY 10011.

Produced by Archetype Press, Inc., Washington, D.C.
Diane Maddex, Project Director
Gretchen Smith Mui and John Hovanec, Editorial Assistants
Robert L. Wiser, Designer

This book was composed in Bernhard Gothic, designed by Lucian Bernhard in 1929 for American Type Founders. The display typography is Wade Sans, designed by Paul Hickson in 1990 for Esselte Letraset.

Printed in Singapore

10   9   8   7   6   5   4   3   2   1

Library of Congress Cataloging-in-Publication Data
Maddex, Diane.
50 favorite furnishings by Frank Lloyd Wright / Diane Maddex.
p.   cm.
Includes bibliographical references and index.
ISBN 0-7651-1670-7 (hardcover)
1. Wright, Frank Lloyd, 1867–1959—Criticism and interpretation.   2. Wright, Frank Lloyd, 1867–1959—Contributions in furniture design.   3. Architect-designed furniture—United States.   I. Wright, Frank Lloyd, 1867–1959.   II. Title.   III. Title: Fifty favorite furnishings by Frank Lloyd Wright.
NK2439.W75M33   1999
749.213—dc21   99-29716
                                                                        CIP

Endpapers and chapter dividers: Adaptation of Design No. 104, a fabric pattern created by Ling Po of Frank Lloyd Wright's office for production by F. Schumacher and Company in 1955. The interlocking spheres and ellipses were inspired by Wright's plans for houses for his sons David and Robert Llewellyn Wright. Drawing by Robert L. Wiser, Archetype Press

Page 2: Spindled chairs and other furnishings from Wright's early career and Prairie-style period on exhibition in a gallery devoted to his work.

INTRODUCTION

The chairs must have been the first thing guests noticed when they walked into Frederick and Lora Robie's dining room in Chicago—as righteous as church pews but so mysterious, their spindled backs screening the table yet inviting tantalizing glimpses of wonders beyond. Nary a Victorian curlicue forced onto the wood, no paint or high finish to hide the proud oak, not a trace of the past in these chairs. In this room, completed in 1910, Frank Lloyd Wright's genius for furnishing a harmonious space is clear. Enclosing the table, the chairs form a room of their own within the larger room. The dining surface is as long and broad as the chairs are tall, but its corner posts mimic the erect chair backs. The ensemble is repeated in miniature in a breakfast nook tucked into the room's projecting bay, where windows with geometric tracery create a screen of light subtly distinguishing inside from outside. A built-in sideboard is the only other furniture to be seen. Most of the decorative flourishes are similarly integrated: lamps atop the table corners with shades reflecting the window patterns; pointed table runners carrying the same diamond shape; wood bands gliding across the ceiling and down the walls to terminate in globes of light; a carpet whose small motif underscores the house's geometry. The Robies were allowed a few personal touches, among them china displayed like art objects on the sideboard's cantilevered ledge. A vase on the dining table holds dried flowers as simple messengers from nature. "If a man has twenty cents for the family meal," Wright said in 1894, "he had best invest three cents of that in a flower; for the glass in the middle of the table the family will be better fed in the long run."

1910 photograph of the Robie House dining room in Chicago

6

This was not his first perfect dining room—the one he designed in 1895 for his own home in Oak Park, Illinois, had led the way—but the Robies' space (completed with the help of George Mann Niedecken) presented one of Wright's most eloquent lessons of what a home should look like inside. Each house, he said then, should be a complete work of art. "It is quite impossible to consider the building one thing and its furnishings another," Wright explained in 1910. The chairs and tables, the windows, the lighting, the objects were "mere structural details" of a building's overall character. Like individual citizens in a democracy, each had its role to play in creating a harmonious union.

Wright (1867–1959) called houses of the day little more than notion stores, bazaars, and junk shops. He was pained when his own clients dragged in furnishings he thought did not belong in his progressive houses, items that were "the horrors of the old order." But at the start of the twentieth century, modern home-owners had few alternatives. So Wright added to his architectural repertoire everything inside a house, even preparing plans showing where furniture was to be placed. He began articulating Wright's rules of domestic order in 1894, restating them in sometimes identical language over the next sixty years:

Furnishings should be seen as parts of the whole composition, not aggregations, "a great thing instead of a collection of smaller ones." A single basic idea—a geometric motif, a plant form—should govern. "Every house worth considering as a

work of art," said Wright, "must have a grammar of its own." Ornament should be integral, arising from the materials and construction themselves. And those materials, chief among them wood, should be limited and natural to be "honest." Natural finishes bring out the nature of materials rather than cover it up as paint would. Natural colors come from the woods and fields—tones of the earth and autumn are "optimistic," in contrast to the "pessimistic" blues, purples, and cold greens "of the ribbon counter." Natural accessories such as simple flowers, dried or fresh, bring the outdoors in. Furniture, heating, lighting, and nearly everything else should be built in as far as possible to make them part of the building. Human scale must be observed. Geometry, with its straight lines conducive to machine manufacture, should prevail. And, said Wright, "above all, integrity," the end product of simplicity and unity.

Wright's principles had many ancestors. As a boy, he learned to revere nature from the Wisconsin landscape and the writings of Emerson and Thoreau. His Unitarian relatives taught him to sanctify unity. His mother introduced him to scale, proportion, and geometry with a set of Froebel kindergarten blocks. His father suggested to him that music was really "an edifice of sound." The twenty-year-old Wright carried these ideas with him when he arrived in Chicago in 1887, eager to build. From Louis Sullivan, his famous mentor and employer from 1888 to 1893, he learned how to mold surfaces as if they were plastic; this was a talent that would aid his furniture making. Once he ventured out on his own in 1893, Wright quickly transformed

Wright's photograph of a living area at Taliesin, rebuilt after a fire in 1914

himself into an organic architect, making buildings grow from nature just as the trees and flowers emerged from the prairie.

To fill his more than five hundred commissions that were built (as many more remained unrealized), Wright needed thousands of furnishings, from chairs and tables to music stands, from art glass to glass mosaics, from carpets to table linens. Many trusted associates served as the "fingers" on his hands, fleshing out an idea or designing items on their own. At his studio in the early days, for instance, he relied heavily on the architect Marion Mahony's exceptional skills to finish furniture and glass designs. During the Prairie years he also called on George Niedecken, an "interior architect" in Milwaukee, to execute furnishings that completed his architectural schemes. Artists such as Richard Bock and Alfonso Iannelli added sculptures and murals, and in Wright's later years his apprentices saw to it that each building was as well dressed inside as outside:

Furniture. Wright himself admitted that he was "black and blue in some spot, somewhere, almost all my life from too intimate contact with my own early furniture." But he kept striving, relying on machine technology to eliminate the fussy joinery and overwrought products of the day. Straight lines, natural markings, and unvarnished finishes became his hallmarks.

These were precepts that others such as the Japanese and Arts and Crafts designers on the Continent and in the United States espoused as well, and it is easy to point out similarities

between their work and Wright's. But Wright helped revolutionize interiors in the way he used his furniture as interior architecture to mark divisions of space. The number of pieces should be limited, he cautioned, with as many as possible built in—at one with the building. Then there was nothing to arrange, nothing to disturb the architect's vision.

Wright's furniture styles evolved from the stolid oak pieces of the Prairie years (1900–17) to the even simpler lines of his Usonian designs (1936–59), which were often of plywood and built by carpenters on site. As late as 1954, when he was eighty-seven, he confided that he thought perfect furniture could be made "someday."

Art Glass. Early on, Wright discovered that glass could be more than merely the "eyes" of a building—it could be the building itself. He used windows to make walls and sometimes ceilings disappear, ushering in light through movable casements, often grouped in expansive bands, or through innovative materials such as Pyrex tubing. Glass was his mirror, as lakes are nature's, and he molded it into screens of light.

The geometrically patterned windows, clerestories, and skylights that Wright designed in the first decade of the twentieth century are among the most beloved of all his furnishings. Infused with the natural colors of the earth, they turned his houses into "shimmering fabrics—woven of rich glass." Sunlight streamed in through them, he said, as if sifted through tree leaves. As building economics changed, he gave them up entirely after the early 1920s. Instead, Wright found other imaginative ways to encase his buildings in crystal.

Decorative Arts. Wright contended that decoration was dangerous in the hands of those who did not understand it. (Everyone else's work was "inferior desecration" to him.) He urged clients to avoid a wagonload of items with no real use and concentrate on "one really fine thing." All ornament had to be integral, growing organically from the building itself.

Mellow walls tinted with autumnal hues took the place of most pictures. Built in even more surely than furniture, they were simply framed, almost like works of art, in wood given the sheen of a flower petal. Wallpaper would only cover a wall's true nature. Carpets on the floors became as much a part of the building as the plaster on the walls. Textiles such as a table scarf clothed a home with a "shimmering robe." Here and there a Japanese print, as an ode to simplicity, or a three-dimensional sculpture provided a key focal point. Such objects might rest on narrow wooden ledges, or decks, that surrounded a room and hid indirect lighting. Nearby, vases held fresh flowers, dried weeds, or tree branches, a sign of nature's lure.

Although all of the fifty furnishings singled out in the following pages are notable in and of themselves, Wright meant each one to be appreciated not in isolation but as an integral component of its own individual space—a part of the building itself.

Wright seated in one of his origami chairs at Taliesin West in 1957

F U R N

When he began his practice of designing furniture about 1895, Wright

adopted the credo of the Arts and Crafts movement: simplicity of design,

natural materials treated naturally, and visible construction methods, pref-

erably turned over to machines. These principles stayed with him even as

the form of his buildings changed during his lifetime. No ornate carvings for

I T U R E

him, no twisted wood, no painted or strained finishes. Beginning with the

spindled tall-back chairs that became his signature, he made his furniture

honest, from assertive tables cantilevered like his houses to office desk sets

striking in their efficiency. Wright excelled at built-in furniture: benches, so-

fas, sideboards, and tables that became an integral part of the architecture.

TALL-BACK CHAIR

Few pieces of furniture are as closely associated with Wright as his tall dining chairs with spindled backs. They epitomize his attempt to bring simplicity and rationality into American households, and they consequently have become icons of modern design. The first tall-back chairs appeared in Wright's own home in Oak Park, Illinois, built in 1889. By 1895, anxious to try out his ever-evolving ideas, the twenty-eight-year-old architect remodeled the family's kitchen into a new dining room and furnished it with a solid oak table, tall chairs with leather seats, built-in cabinets, recessed lighting, and windows of his own creation. The ensemble, clothed in the colors of a prairie autumn, was hailed by the new *House Beautiful* magazine in 1897 and again in 1899, when its furniture was singled out for being "in perfect harmony with the room." Wright himself began to assert that any freestanding furniture should possess the attributes of a house's built-ins and "should be seen as a minor part of the building itself." Originally the chair backs, which rise to playful round finials, were lined with rows of ball chains. Wright eventually changed these to squared spindles of oak and flared the rear legs. Encircling the table, the chairs screen out distractions, concentrating the diners' attention on the task at hand. Moving the spindles to the sides, the architect miniaturized his vision into a high chair for his son Llewellyn in 1902. For each family member, the chairs helped induce good posture if not the moral rectitude they seem to imply. Wright returned over and over to this chair design throughout his lifetime, extending the spindles down to the floor, up to the top rail, and along the sides and using different materials and bolder strokes. A vertical link to the earth, each one of them firmly anchored the sitter. Although one boy later recalled the "unequalled agony of sitting" in the Robie House dining chairs, this design became one of Wright's most dramatic signatures—mere board transformed into an abstract version of lace, light and dark, there and not there.

15

HUSSER DINING SET

Continuing to experiment with his tall-back dining chairs, Wright in 1899 designed a masterful oak dining set for Helen and Joseph Husser in Chicago. Wright found it maddening, from a design standpoint, that humans had to sit, but if they had to sit anywhere he preferred the dining room because its furniture was much more "easily managed in the architecture," he confessed in 1910. His dining table and chairs for the Hussers held center stage in an octagonal dining bay that projected out to frame a private view of Lake Michigan. Although the house was demolished in 1926, the dining room furniture has survived. The Hussers could choose from not one but three dining tables and twenty-four chairs designed to be combined for entertaining. To elongate the line of the chair backs, Wright dropped the spindles nearly to the floor, terminating them in a small band that wraps around the legs. A gentle curve begins at the terminals and wends its way down to the rear feet. The back still begins in a deep crest rail, like the chairs in Wright's own home, but he would soon eliminate this in favor of a simple line of spindles from top to bottom. The effect recalls Japanese screens and woodwork, motifs that also inspired English Arts and Crafts designers of the time. Carved with a woven-wood border, the table soars over its spindled base in a dramatic cantilever that hints at the Prairie houses and, later, the world-famous Fallingwater still to come from Wright's drafting board. Built-in lamps over flower holders originally lighted the four corners of the table, a device that Wright would use as well on tables in his houses for the Martins (1904) in Buffalo, New York, the Robies (1908) in Chicago, the Mays (1908) in Grand Rapids, Michigan, and the Boyntons (1908) in Rochester, New York. With chairs pulled up close to screen the diners and soft lights glowing at each corner, this dining ensemble was a smaller-scaled room within a room.

SLANT-BACK CHAIR

In 1901 Wright set himself clearly apart from English Arts and Crafts designers who extolled the satisfactions of handmade furnishings. Wright embraced their fondness for a simple life in harmony with nature, but for him the future lay in modern technology, not in medieval handicraft. In a speech entitled "The Art and Craft of the Machine," the young architect called machines the artist's "best friend." Their gift, he said, was to free wood to be wood and to allow "the poor as well as the rich [to] enjoy beautiful surface treatments of clean, strong forms...." Wright soon added to his repertoire a slant-back chair exemplifying these ideals. Paying homage to a machine's ability to produce perfect lines, a spare oak board slides past a simple leather seat down to the rear stretcher to support the sitter's back at just the right angle. It peeks provocatively above the stiles, which are cuffed with rectangular blocks top and bottom. The act of sitting is reduced to its most basic elements—creating almost "a machine to sit in," as Wright in 1931 described the first step in furniture design. The chair shown here dates from about 1904 and was in Wright's own home, which often became the repository for copies of client designs that he particularly liked. Similar examples appeared about the same time at his aunts' Hillside Home School (1887) in Spring Green, Wisconsin, without the bottom cuffs; at the Little House (1902) in Peoria, Illinois, with a rectangular back perforation and low, slanted stiles; at Unity Temple (1905) in Oak Park; and at the Robie House (1908) in Chicago. At the Larkin Administration Building (1903) in Buffalo, New York, some of these chairs offered an arm rest for stenographers, others had short, capped stiles for the dining room, and still others came with a truncated back. Apparently inspired by Wright, the Dutchman Gerrit Rietveld built his startling Red-Blue Chair in 1920, in which the seat and back planes are even more exaggerated to eliminate all need for applied ornament—achieving an almost fully reclining position, which Wright found to be the only "attractive posture of relaxation."

18

PRINT TABLE

After Commodore Matthew Perry helped open Japan to trade with the West in 1854, many Americans became infatuated with a culture that until then had been relatively unknown to them. As a young architect in Chicago in the 1890s, Wright was one of them. He was inspired by Japanese buildings, and he soon became a collector of Japanese woodblock prints, a hobby that intensified after his first trip to Japan in 1905. To him, these prints distilled the essence of modernity. In his *Autobiography* of 1932, he praised them as a democratic art form that eliminated "the insignificant, a process of simplification in art in which I was engaged...." Although he was frequently financially pressed into using his prints as barter and he often sold them outright for the income, Wright loved to display his *ukiyo-e* at home and urged his clients to show them as well. He thus designed an ingenious folding print table for this purpose. A poplar-and-pine version standing about four feet tall was made for the Oak Park house around 1895. Others were installed in Susan Lawrence Dana's 1902 house in Springfield, Illinois (opposite), and in the Little House of 1903 in Peoria, Illinois. To display prints, spindled sides were swung out to support a broad, hinged table top, one side of which could be tilted up. When not in use, the print table was folded up into a compact H-shaped unit, its two-sided top lowered between posts underneath. Wright also designed a narrow, spindled mahogany print stand and used it in 1908 to exhibit his Japanese print collection at the Art Institute of Chicago. Every furniture designer of the day, Wright believed, mistreated wood—except the Japanese. His print tables, with their evocation of Japanese screens, paid tribute both to that country's respect for natural materials and to its esteemed art. Toward the end of his life, Wright insisted that he looked to Japan more for its prints than for its architecture. When he died in 1959, his collection included this woodblock print (c. 1853) by Ando Hiroshige (left) among some six thousand others—probably less than half the number he had amassed.

LARKIN DESK SET

Always the innovator, Wright in 1903 designed a futuristic office building for the Larkin Company in Buffalo, New York, and filled it with equally forward-looking furniture. Here Wright rejected architecture's "old order" and replaced it from the walls in with a completely coordinated business environment. Workers in this mail-order company offering soap and household products toiled in and around a wide-open, sun-filled interior court. Little did customers know that as the employees worked, they sat and tallied orders on some of the earliest metal office furniture. It was the perfect choice for the building Wright called "a great fire-proof vault." Everything in it was designed for safety, efficiency, durability, cleanliness, and comfort, down to the workspace of the most junior clerk. One of Wright's most imaginative designs was a metal desk with a swing-out chair: at night, the back folded down and the unit could be tucked into the kneehole to allow mops to glide underneath without obstruction. On top of the desk was a layer of magnesite, a vinyl-like compound of wood and concrete that was poured on to create an indestructible surface (it was also used for flooring). Executives directed the business from painted steel armchairs with leather seats. The rectangular back tilted and provided ventilation through a perforated pattern of squares. Under a swiveling seat, the cruciform base sat on casters for easy movement. Elsewhere, built-in metal file cabinets and wall-hung toilets proclaimed a new age in office design. The Larkin Administration Building lasted only until 1950, when it came down, but Wright's ideas for open workplaces with custom furnishings have lived on.

MARTIN BARREL CHAIR

Turning from clean right angles to the curves that enchanted him into the 1950s, Wright produced one of his most successful and sophisticated chairs about 1904 for Isabel and Darwin Martin of Buffalo, New York. A few years earlier he had designed a low, octagonal barrel-style chair for the Bradley House in Kankakee, Illinois, an effort that was soon modified with spindled sides for Susan Lawrence Dana in Springfield and the Francis Littles in Peoria. But for the magnificent Martin House, home to the secretary of the Larkin Company, Wright found the perfect form to address the "unfortunate necessity" of sitting. A round, padded seat cantilevers out from a semi-circle of oak spindles, recalling his earliest chairs. At arm height, the screen turns into a solid back and majestically flares out and back, tapering toward the edges. On the sides the wood rises slightly to cradle the sitter's arms. Matthews Bros. Manufacturing Company of Milwaukee made and shipped about eight of these chairs for the living and dining rooms and the library, where they could work as architectural ensembles. In the living room, a pair flanked a high-back settle, offering a circular counterpoint to the otherwise rectilinear lines and matching ball sconces above. When Wright visited the house in 1936, he became so enamored of his own early work that he decided to refine the Martin barrel chair for his second home at Taliesin in Spring Green, Wisconsin. He also specified it for two of his new commissions: Fallingwater (1935) in Mill Run, Pennsylvania, and Wingspread (1937), outside Racine, Wisconsin. In those, the rotund seats extended beneath the wood frame to approximate a globe, bringing Wright's spherical play full circle.

ROBIE SOFA

In the midst of designing the Robie House in Chicago—one of his most assured Prairie-style homes—Wright abruptly left the country in the fall of 1909 to work on a German publication that would tell the world about his revolutionary work. He took with him his mistress, Mamah Borthwick Cheney, and did not return for a year. The task of completing the Robie furnishings fell to George Mann Niedecken, the "interior architect" from Milwaukee with whom Wright had worked first in 1904 and then more regularly after 1907. Niedecken filled the forty-four-foot-long living room with a geometrically patterned carpet and gave the Robies a unique red oak sofa with built-in elements, one of several unusual combination units to appear in Wright houses. Eliminating the need for side tables (which owners might move around to suit themselves), the architectonic sofa bears wide arms that spread outward like wings and connect with a narrower wood shelf, or console, at the back. A separate rear table was thus also made redundant. Wood strips along the edges and sides emphasize the cantilevered effect and mirror the horizontal layering of the house itself. Wright liked to use built-in furniture to organize and simplify a space—creating "complete harmony, nothing to arrange, nothing to disturb: room and furniture an 'entity.'" In reality built-ins let the architect control the look of a room by foreclosing homeowners' individual tastes, which from time to time conflicted with Wright's. The Robie furnishings, for which Niedecken billed them directly, included a small footstool, called a tabouret, that could double as a table; its feet flare outward in imitation of the sofa legs. A tall-back chair appears in yet another guise: with upholstery, rather than spindles, to comfort the sitter's back. It is not as dramatic as the house's dining chairs, whose spindles cascade from the crest rail to the floor (page 6), but its stiles are capped with blocks that could grace a throne. The space is pulled together with wood ceiling bands that stretch from side to side and art glass windows with stylized prairie flowers framing motifs representing the house's own geometry.

27

COONLEY DESK

As he did with a large handful of Wright's other complex Prairie houses, George Mann Niedecken took charge of seeing that the interiors of the Coonley House in Riverside, Illinois, were furnished to Wright's specifications. A small desk for the rear guest room obviously struck his fancy, for about 1910 he made a presentation drawing of it as poignant as a Japanese print. Not even four feet tall or wide, this charming nook that invites letter writing synthesizes the key design features of the house. Its white oak writing surface boldly cantilevers outward to recall Wright's Prairie houses. Rectangles within rectangles on the doors bring to mind the outswinging windows and the geometric tiles that enliven the facade. Door and drawer pulls underscore the square motif. Hipped metal-and-glass lamp shades resemble the roofs overhead. It is a gem of a piece, just one small item in a significant house once filled with furniture of all kinds, a mural by Niedecken, carpets, tableware, and monogrammed linens. Said Wright, "I put the best in me into the Coonley House." So did Niedecken, who completed the furnishings during Wright's year-long absence. The desk, which was manufactured by the Niedecken-Walbridge Company in Milwaukee, must have been one of the interior designer's own favorites: similar pieces have turned up in the Midwest, indicating that Niedecken adapted this sturdy design for some of his own later clients.

IRVING TABLE-COUCH

A desk of a different sort was made for the house of Edward and Florence Irving in Decatur, Illinois. One of the projects orphaned when Wright departed for Europe in 1909, it was left in the hands of Hermann von Holst, who in turn called on one of Wright's ablest employees to help him. Marion Mahony, an architect, had joined Wright's office in 1895 and spent the next fourteen years preparing exquisite presentation drawings and assisting Wright with designs for his furnishings. George Mann Niedecken joined her in executing the Irving furnishings. A skilled designer well versed in progressive interiors, European and American, Niedecken—like Mahony—could almost read Wright's mind when it came to fleshing out the furnishings. Mahony, however, asserted that the conception of the Irving furnishings rested with her. The unique table-couch-desk-lamp combination created for the living room fits perfectly into the Wrightian system of built-ins that mark interior architectural boundaries. Placed close to the fireplace, with its sumac and prairie-flower mural by Niedecken, the couch would have allowed one of the residents to lounge against pillows or sit beneath a large box of a lamp (now lost), while another could work at the oak fall-front desk secluded in the pier. On the dramatically cantilevered table sat a custom-designed lamp. Either separately or together, the Irvings would have been able to enjoy the fire, not to mention the satisfaction of using a piece of furniture so thoughtfully crafted. Planes intersect freely, and light meets dark, much like the fireplace and the exterior of the house, one of a trio bearing Mahony's mark in the small Millikin Place community.

GREENE SETTLE

Toward the end of his Prairie years, after he returned from his sojourn in Europe, Wright in 1912 designed a wood-trimmed cube of a house in Aurora, Illinois, and placed in it one of his most assertive freestanding sofas. Unlike his early high-back, high-sided settles in the Dana and Martin Houses and the Robie sofa, with its low back and roomy arms, this piece for the Greene family resurrects the spindles with which Wright launched his career in furnishings. A screen of oak surrounds the settle on three sides, while the leather seat pushes out past the arms in a subtle cantilever. One or more cushions probably filled the back, although the settle's good bones show well without adornment. Rails running atop the spindles and beneath the seat intersect with simple post legs, which stop at broad, square front feet that visually carry the settle's weight. Wright did not like to acknowledge many sources of inspiration, but the Greene settle bears at least a family resemblance to one promoted by Gustav Stickley in a 1901 issue of his *Craftsman* magazine. The great Arts and Crafts furniture maker's piece, however, was no match for the master's later creation. Wright called Mission furniture "crude," its plainness a far cry from the simplicity achieved in his own work. While Stickley's settle needed to rest on six legs, Wright's made do with four. Stickley raised his frame well off the ground, whereas Wright lowered his to within touching distance of the floor. And although Stickley had to add a vertical support at the back for his spindles, Wright created a wide, unbroken screen. Not a single line is out of place. Form and function are one, as Wright said they should be.

MIDWAY DINING SET

By 1913 Wright had essentially abandoned the ground-hugging Prairie houses that had sustained him for the past decade and began to write a new chapter in his practice. That year an opportunity came his way to design an indoor-outdoor entertainment complex in Chicago to rival the joyful beer gardens of Europe. At Midway Gardens, developed by the son of a former client on the midway of the 1893 World's Columbian Exposition, Wright was able to surround his architecture with music, and he played many variations on what was to become a lifelong theme of circles. Above doors in the tavern, colored bubbles floated across wall murals, bumping into each other in sheer delight. Clustered globes of light hung down or were hoisted by stylized statues. And to go with them Wright planned sprightly metal dining chairs with discs for the backs and seats. For these and other features at Midway, Wright turned to his "trusty T Square and aspiring triangle." Tapping out a counterpoint to the two linked circles on each chair, triangles step down the back and enlarge themselves below in steel to form the legs. They would not have looked out of place at a stylish neighborhood soda fountain. Neither these nor matching tables were ever built, however, because Midway Gardens never had the financial backing it needed. The popular center closed in 1916 and was torn down in 1929. Wright's metal dining set, with solid chair backs, was first made in the 1960s for use in the Fellowship dining room at Taliesin West, his home in Scottsdale, Arizona. As on the chairs, triangles support the base of the table, a reproduction of which is now manufactured with either the originally planned square top or a circular one that replays the chair's theme. Wright's designs for lamps, dishes, and even beer mugs were made in Midway's short life—all that was missing were the Wright tabletops on which to put them.

MORI CHAIR

Wright's affinity for Japan stood him in good stead when he was called on in 1914 to design an oriental art shop in Chicago for Shigehisa Mori, an art dealer. His shop was one of three commercial spaces Wright transformed in the Fine Arts Building, where Wright himself had a studio for a time in 1908 and 1910. The cubic chairs installed in the shop were as sparely drawn as one of the Japanese woodblock prints Wright so admired. A dozen years earlier he had exhibited at the Chicago Architectural Club another cube chair from his studio that was more daringly modern but certainly less Japanese. The Mori chairs, made of oak with drop-in seats covered in leather, seem as square as boxes, which is what the exhibited chairs were. Subtle touches, however, make this an illusion. The rear stiles are set in to meet the seat back, whereas the front stiles slide by at the sides. It is the top line—arms that meld into a back rail—that carries through the seat's square motif. The arms gracefully cantilever over the seat, which floats forward beyond the line of the front stiles and the bottom stretchers. The Mori shop was closed in 1922, and its other furnishings, including cabinets and tables, were dispersed. The chairs here are shown in front of the fireplace in Wright's Oak Park drafting room, where, not far from the earlier cube chairs, they help illustrate his genius at turning a few simple sticks of wood into an understated masterpiece.

37

IMPERIAL CHAIR

One of Wright's most important commissions, the Imperial Hotel in Tokyo, has now vanished except for some furniture and ruins of the lobby that have been reconstructed at an outdoor museum. The sprawling, three-story hotel, reached only by long train and boat trips from Wright's home, challenged all of his skills for eight years beginning in 1915. He responded with an ode to a country he greatly admired, filled with sculpted stone walls, murals, and an astonishing array of public and guest room furnishings, all infused with geometric legerdemain as only Wright could do it. On its opening day in 1923, the Imperial suffered–but survived–a massive earthquake that destroyed lesser buildings. It stood through World War II but fell to "progress" in 1968. A few oak chairs from the hotel's promenade, covered with more recent upholstery, made it to safety. With their hexagonal backs, they mimic the peaked rise of the ceiling in the "peacock alley" and the shape of its uppermost panels. Braces along the sides repeat the six-sided motif. Photographs show earlier chairs like these with caned seats, backs, and side panels. Both types fit neatly around octagonal tables. For Midway Gardens in Chicago, Wright had specified larger hexagonal-back chairs with short, angled "wings" in lieu of arms. Lack of money prevented their manufacture then, but an almost identical version shows up in a photograph of an Imperial bedroom, reinforcing the hexagonal theme introduced downstairs. Wright often found inventive ways of shuffling the deck he was dealt.

HOLLYHOCK SOFA

During their protracted effort to build her a house in
Hollywood, Aline Barnsdall begged Wright to "please do as
wonderful a thing with the inside of my house as ... with the
outside." He did, despite being in Japan much of the time to
direct work on the Imperial Hotel. He left supervision of the
plans in the hands of his son Lloyd and the Austrian émigré
Rudolph M. Schindler. When Hollyhock House, as it was
nicknamed, was ready for Barnsdall in 1921, some extraordinary
fittings awaited her. Many rooms blossomed with hollyhocks,
her favorite flower—molded in art stone, stylized in art glass,
and carved in wood on chairs. In the living room she found
an imaginative group resembling built-in furniture (now
reconstructed) that was placed not along the walls but at the
heart of the space, encircling an octagonal hearth. An oak sofa
is combined with two tables plus a torchère on either side of
a narrow aisle, each section angled to surround the fireplace—
fulfilling the same idea behind the inglenooks in his early
houses. Spindled chairs, some with high backs and some with
low backs, pull up to desklike tables on four sides. Like leggy
hollyhocks, the lamps stretch seven feet toward the ceiling
and cast their light from upturned, etched pyramids. (Somewhat simpler torchères also appeared in the lobby and
bedrooms of Tokyo's Imperial Hotel, which Wright was then
building.) Water flowed in front of the fire over golden tiles,
a tone repeated in the walls and two built-in Japanese
screens. Hardly just a room within a room, the novel furniture
group was more an island in a world of Wright's making.

HOLLYHOCK DINING SET

The best dining room, suggested Wright, is a "bright, cozy, cheerful place you involuntarily enter with a smile." From the entry hall of Hollyhock House in Hollywood, the dining room beckons just four steps up. This serene area, as small as the living room is large, is set aside like a serving platter. Beaded panels of white mahogany wrap the walls, one of Wright's rare concessions to a client. Clerestories interrupt the wood to draw light down into the room; below them, asymmetrical pieces of purple glass in casement windows mediate between outside and inside. At the center of the room are more holly-hocks to please Aline Barnsdall. Along a trellis of stepping squares they climb the backs of a half dozen ingenious seats— a twist on Wright's classic tall chairs—and poke above the crest. Falling straight to the floor, the decorative back takes the place of rear legs . An unusual triangular pedestal on the table repeats the abstract pattern and holds aloft a hexagonal top; below is a rotated hexagonal base. Squares, triangles, hexagons—the geometry of the house came together supremely in its furniture. For Wright, arranging people around a dining table was much easier than accommodating their diverse activities in living rooms or elsewhere in the house. Dining, he said in 1931, "always was a great artistic opportunity."

FALLINGWATER BUILT-INS

As Wright suggested early in his career, as much furniture as possible should be built in as part of the architecture. The idea was not new, but he carried it out to perfection in order to unify the design, conserve space, reduce the number of furnishings, and, not insignificantly, control how his clients lived. Ample window seats, he said, did away with the need for chairs, which only cluttered up a room. By the mid-1930s, when Wright designed his world-famous Fallingwater, lifestyles were becoming more informal and servants were less frequently available to take care of housework. The weekend retreat planned for Edgar and Liliane Kaufmann in Mill Run, Pennsylvania, in 1935 had to be especially carefree. Built-ins abound, from bedrooms and guest rooms to the kitchen, dining area, and, most spectacularly, the forty-eight-foot-long living room, much of them made by the Gillen Woodwork Corporation of Milwaukee. Sofas designed as simple slashes cantilever out from the sandstone walls, their beige upholstery harmonizing with the stone itself. They cleverly hide indirect lighting and radiators. Bands veneered in black walnut run along the bottom and lead the eye toward tables, and then square footstools, in the same rich material. Tabletops with subtly rounded edges also cantilever over their bases just as Wright's masterpiece spreads its arms out to the rocky waterfall below. Stepping down from low to lower to nearly the floor, these small freestanding pieces of furniture mirror the architectural dynamism outside. Bright pillows on the window seats and cushions in the wood-framed footstools, like fallen leaves in an autumn forest, bring nature's colors into the house.

JOHNSON WAX DESK

The office revolution Wright launched with the Larkin Building at the turn of the century was won three decades later at the S. C. Johnson Administration Building in Racine, Wisconsin, begun in 1936. For this manufacturer of Johnson Wax, Wright produced a low, red brick building with sinuous curves that telegraphed the essence of modernity. In the Great Workroom, a refinement of the Larkin Building's innovative interior court, rows of tall, pale columns taper upward from slender feet to hold broad disks—they have been compared to lily pads, but the effect is much more akin to a forest shaded by leafy canopies. Rays from the skylights break through the "boughs" to dapple the workers below. As they have since the building was opened in 1939, employees sit at desks designed to harmonize with the architecture. Wright again turned to metal for efficiency, this time to tubular steel that was rounded like the building's own outline. Drawers as red as the brick outside swing forward, and a wastebasket hangs clear of the floor. Above them, parallel maple desktops seem to float in midair. Circles reappear in the chair, spiraling down from disks that form the pivoting back and the seat to rest on an offset half circle lined with red tubes. Not only do they match the desk's side supports, they also mimic the novel Pyrex tubing that lights much of the building. Wright allowed only three legs on the secretarial chairs, requiring the sitters to add their own two feet for balance. Executives were permitted to have four steady legs on their chairs, and other variations in the furniture were used to fit office duties and changing requirements over the years. With its cheerful color, streamlined shapes, and materials that the Bauhaus would have approved, the modular furniture in this early open-office environment was as important as any brick in the building.

TALIESIN DINING SET

Change and adaptation, adaptation and refinement—only by constant tinkering did Wright test his ideas and inch toward perfection. The dining area of his second home, Taliesin, in Spring Green, Wisconsin, served as one of his architectural laboratories. Spurred in part by necessity—calamitous fires in 1914 and 1925—he reworked the space and furnishings over nearly a half century. At first, after the limestone house was begun in 1911, severely rectilinear plank chairs not much taller than the dining table were paired with spare benches. After the 1914 fire, the chairs became more complex: square in shape with broad oak arms, a broad crest rail, an open back, intricate interlocking rear stiles, and padded seats. Replaced again after the 1925 fire, Wright's new chairs were more delicate but still spartan, featuring side panels and a deep, tilted crest rail, both in plywood to frame an open back and an upholstered seat; they were joined by several tall-back spindled chairs similar to the Robie dining chairs from two decades earlier, with the addition of arms, a slanted crest rail between clipped wings, and an oversize scale fit for a giant. In 1936 Wright reached further back into his store of early furniture designs when he rediscovered the barrel chair made about 1904 for Isabel and Darwin Martin of Buffalo, New York. He decided to make a new version for Wingspread, the house he began designing in 1937 for the Herbert Johnson family near Racine, Wisconsin. Made of plywood and chestnut, rather than oak as originally, the chair arms did not rise upward, the crest flared less, and the seat bottom was rounded to a semicircle. Wright placed a set of these modernized chairs around his table at Taliesin, the base of which is spindled like the chairs. What was once all angles is now full of curves, the barrel chairs forming a scalloped edge around a golden sea of rectangles.

50

CANTILEVERED DESK

Although so much of Wright's furniture changed—and improved—over the years, one item did not need much refinement. His tables remained basically as they started in his 1895 dining room in Oak Park, with just a few minor variations on his one great theme: the cantilever, which he regarded as "the most romantic, most free, of all principles of construction." Showing the daring that characterized his whole career, tabletops from the very beginning soared out over modest bases to provide unobstructed platforms for dining, writing, or temporarily resting coffee cups and magazines. The desk in his own bedroom-study at Taliesin in Wisconsin follows this functional form. A broad expanse of plywood rests on a simple wooden cube. The cantilever metaphor—bringing to mind the overhanging roofs of his Prairie houses and the outstretched terraces of Fallingwater— is amplified here with lower pieces that fit under the wings of the desktop. At the front is a square, two-level coffee table similar to others Wright designed in the 1930s, its four slat legs moved from the corners to the center of each side like the filling in a sandwich. A cantilevered credenza and a cruciform table tuck under the opposite edges. Between them rests a low, overstuffed ottoman. The dynamic planes jut forward and recede, rise up and settle down gently. And in the command chair, its rotund lines matched only by the glass vase, sat Wright.

TALIESIN WEST CHAIRS

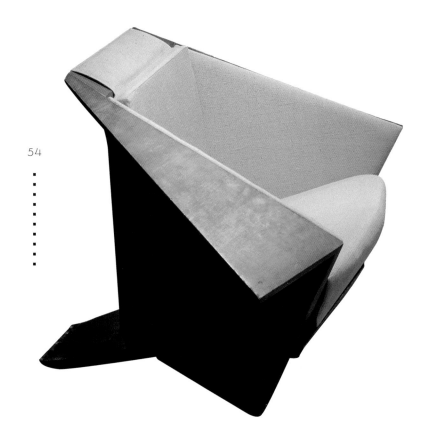

Wright liked to call concrete the "gutter rat" of building materials, and he reveled in raising it above its lowly origins. When it came to furniture, plywood occupied the same place in his bag of tricks. Contemporaries of Wright also took up plywood in the 1930s and 1940s, compressing it, molding it, and stretching it as far as new technologies would take it. But Wright was already expert at building furniture with plywood. Because it was inexpensive and could be assembled by the carpenters on site, it became part of the grammar of his Usonian houses. Conjuring up the image of a Japanese artist deftly folding paper into delicate origami, Wright in 1937 created one of his most famous chairs for use at Taliesin. Like a butterfly with wings poised for flight, the origami chair, said Wright, helped make sitters look graceful in spite of themselves. The arms of the Taliesin chairs had cutouts recalling his wood screens, but other versions such as those designed for Taliesin West after 1946 were solid and narrower (left). Today these folded butterflies brought down to earth fill the living room of Wright's winter home in Scottsdale, Arizona, begun in 1937. Just beyond, in a room called the cove (opposite), is a set of equally inventive plywood chairs placed around a hexagonal table identical to ones in the living room. Wrapped in a playful jumble of shapes, these seats seem almost anthropomorphic, like many of Wright's chairs.

USONIAN BUILT-INS

Wright turned to built-in furniture for his own 1889 home in Oak Park and continued to specify it throughout the rest of his life's work. It made the furnishings an extension of the architecture, helped coordinate materials and colors, and limited homeowners' sometimes inappropriate choices—built-ins were simplicity itself. As at Fallingwater, living room sofas were excellent candidates for this treatment. Pushed against a wall, they became background items, clearing the foreground for selected accent tables, side chairs, and footstools. Space and money were both at a premium in the Usonian houses that Wright designed beginning in the mid-1930s, so built-ins again became his solution. In the 1950 house of Mary and William Palmer of Ann Arbor, Michigan, a built-in sofa holds the prime spot next to the fireplace. Autumn gold cushions fill a frame of the same cypress that lines the walls and rises to the center point of the peaked ceiling. Behind are cantilevered shelves that serve as a divider, and below is a triangular table that snuggles up close to the sofa. The triangle, in fact, is the module, or plan, around which the house was conceived. More tables carry out the motif, and the waxed red floor underneath is inscribed to underscore the grand plan. Pale green footstools—triangles, of course—can be rearranged as needed not just for comfort and extra seating but also to extend the geometric possibilities of the space. Even the lighting was planned in advance and built in: hidden behind wood decks to bathe the room in a soft, diffused glow.

MUSIC STAND

Next to a built-in sofa, music was a necessity for Wright. Wherever he looked he found, or created, affinities between music and architecture. "The symphony, as my father first taught me, is an edifice of sound," the architect wrote in his 1932 *Autobiography*. Wright built buildings with visual rhythm and harmony and used mathematical systems not unlike those on which Beethoven based a piano sonata. Architecture was the superior art, he suggested, but noted that the "idiosyncrasy of the client does not exist for the great composer," nor does he have to worry about utilitarian needs and the laws of physics as do the great architects. Wright was happy to share his own love of Beethoven, Bach, and Mozart with his clients, even the idiosyncratic ones. In addition to theaters, churches, and other public venues for music, Wright designed a number of residential spaces for musical owners: a living room that doubled as a concert hall for one, a musicians' balcony for another. But for the compact Usonian house of Isadore and Lucille Zimmerman of Manchester, New Hampshire, he could fit in little more than a piano and a handsome music stand. The couple had admired the quartet stands he had devised in the mid-1940s for Taliesin's living room and its Hillside Playhouse, so when he designed their house in 1950 he gave them one of their own. A far cry from the typical, unstable metal stand, Wright's creation calls attention to the importance of music, not to mention his own ingenuity. Four broad ledges, joined with a triangular motif, amply support the musicians' scores in front of coordinated stools. Above the stand, a cap hipped like one of Wright's roofs hides indirect lights. Space was even allowed on top for plants—nature, music, and architecture all brought together in one perfect composition.

59

LOVNESS DINING SET

Wright's tall-back chairs took many forms during the seven decades of his career, but—with perhaps one exception—none were as exotic as the ones built by Donald and Virginia Lovness for their lakeside cottage in Stillwater, Minnesota. The chairs are especially unusual here in the northern woods because they were originally intended for the sunny hillside in Hollywood, California, on which Wright built Hollyhock House for Aline Barnsdall in 1921. Instead, another chair motif with stylized hollyhocks was used. The two designs are standouts in Wright's great panoply of dining chairs. Salvaged from potential oblivion, the set in the Lovness cottage was fabricated in 1972, almost two decades after the couple began their main house in 1955. Along the layered oak backs, three squares upended to form diamonds range along a background of half octagons on either side—allusions to the octagonal fireplace and the square patterns that energize Hollyhock House. Wrightian red cushions, made by Virginia Lovness, are attached with tasseled ties that cascade down the backs, a feature used on earlier Wright chairs. The table edges and the sides of the base pick up the chairs' geometric theme. Placed between a generous built-in sideboard and a hanging pole lamp of Wright's design, the set has taken on a woodsy, organic quality and made itself right at home here.

RAYWARD FURNITURE

Although Wright liked to view each house as a unique commission, he sometimes made his work easier by recycling some old favorites among his furniture designs—perhaps modifying them, perhaps not. In 1955, when he designed Tirranna for the John L. Rayward family of New Canaan, Connecticut, Wright was eighty-eight years old. Sixty years' worth of tables and chairs were behind him, and he brought some of them back to life here. Bright nesting tables used in the living room (below) were first tried out at Taliesin West about 1937. Crisply geometric, they feature a hexagonal top paired with its shadow; a bottom shelf is held in place by three slat legs that form a triangular base. Nearby were low plywood side chairs with gently rounded, spindled backs and flared arms—designs similar to chairs used in the 1930s and adapted in the 1950s . For the Raywards' oak dining table, Wright produced a set of similar side chairs whose angled plank legs are joined by a stretcher with triangular cutouts (pages 64–65). Compared to Wright's more traditional tall spindled

dining chairs, these seats with low curved backs are conspicuously dainty. The house was later furnished with dining chairs from the first commercial line of Wright's furniture launched in 1955 by the Heritage-Henredon Furniture Company. Another variation on the Robie chair theme was also made for the Raywards. With solid panels beneath the seat, sculptural molding, and a deep crest rail, it looked satisfyingly substantial. In addition, at some point some of Wright's most unusual tall-back chairs were moved into the house (opposite), but it is unclear where these might have been used. A solid plank of oak rises from the floor and tapers toward the head. Five triangles march down in descending order, pointing on the back to a triangular buttress. It is no-nonsense seating but regal in its conception. This same chair design is known to have been placed in houses for the Davis family (1950) of Marion, Indiana, and the Ablins (1958) of Bakersfield, California. Beginning with his own dining room in 1895, the high-back chair remained a staple of Wright's furniture vocabulary for his entire lifetime.

ART

Glass was Wright's métier, and he used it boldly to furnish his buildings with light, pattern, and color. Not much else mattered as much in his early commissions—one might do without a chair or a table by Wright but not, especially in the Prairie years, without his windows. They broke down solid walls into "limpid surfaces" like water in the landscape, he said. As screens

GLASS

of glass, often grouped innovatively in broad bands, they coaxed the outside in. Geometric motifs abstracted from nature reinforced that link and brought joy from morning to evening, as light changed the colored glass and swept floors and ceilings with patterns and shadows. Throughout his long life, Wright continued to experiment with glass—his favorite building material.

ROBERTS WINDOW

The art glass for which Wright is renowned today did not rise up from his drafting board fully conceived. It took a few years—not many, to be sure—for him to perfect the form that homeowners coveted and other designers envied. For his remodeled dining room of 1895 (page 14), Wright simply adapted a lotus design from a pattern book to bathe the room in the mystique of Egypt. The next year he produced a far more elaborate window in the stair hall of a house he remodeled for the Charles Roberts family in Oak Park. Wright's debt to his mentor, Louis Sullivan, seems clear. Under his *Lieber Meister*'s tutelage from 1888 to 1893, the young architect absorbed Sullivan's fluid style of portraying nature. The Roberts window is Sullivanesque ornament transferred to glass. Like a floral bouquet, petals spread gracefully across the arch and drift down into the center "stem." Segmented circles touch and overlap—even forming lotus patterns here and there. Smaller windows in the study and elsewhere repeat the main theme. Some of the details may be transitional in style and the whole may owe a debt to Sullivan, but Wright's growing ability to control light and views is as clear as glass. Speaking in 1928 about its magic, Wright said that "we can think of uses to which it might be put as various and beautiful as the frost designs upon the pane of glass itself." This early piece of window wizardry must still have been fresh in his mind.

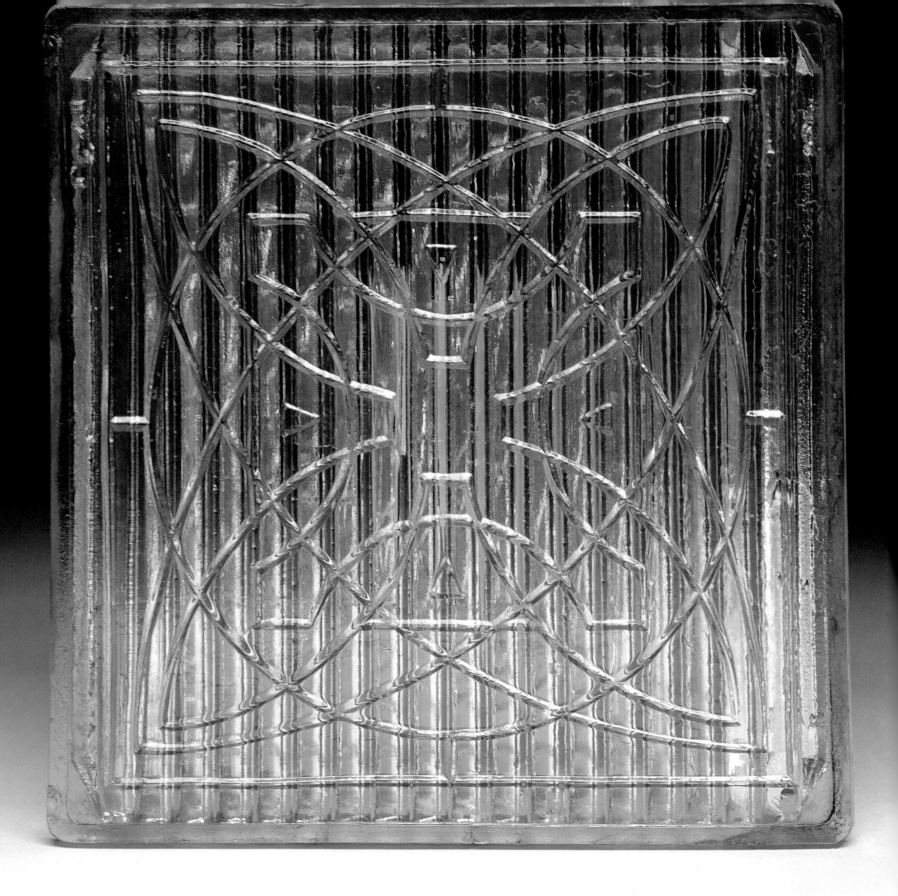

LUXFER PRISM GLASS

Wright was not done with his compass, although he was soon to put it aside in favor of a T-square for his glass designs. Circular forms reappeared in 1897 on an innovative glass block he designed—and patented, guaranteeing him enough income to add a studio to his Oak Park home. In the years before electricity, the far reaches of offices, stores, basements, ships, and similar spaces could be dark. For decades inventors had been seeking a way to bring in more light. Prismatic glass, inspired by the Fresnel lenses in lighthouses, became the answer. Ribs of triangular prisms on the backs of molded, four-inch glass blocks directed the light where it was needed, providing up to fifty times as much light as plate glass. Rows of blocks were placed in grids and electroglazed to make them watertight and fireproof. In an 1894 design competition Wright drew the entire facade of an office building using prismatic glass (never built), but the blocks were more typically installed in transoms or on sidewalks. The American Luxfer Prism Company, the industry leader that was owned by some Wright clients, lost little time in asking the up-and-coming architect to design blocks for the firm (whose name meant "to carry light" in Latin). Although Wright eventually created and patented about forty plate and prism designs, the one most frequently produced was this Sullivanesque pattern from 1897. A square-within-a-square motif frames the four-inch block and encloses a circle and a swirl of ellipses—flattened circles—that collide like atoms. Luxfer prisms were a great commercial success, but by the 1920s and 1930s they faded in importance as electricity became widespread. Wright is not known to have installed any of them in his own buildings.

STUDIO WINDOW

Using money earned from his Luxfer prism glass, Wright
in 1898 built a complete studio adjacent to his home in Oak
Park. To the left of the reception hall is a two-story drafting
room, to the right an octagonal library in which he met clients.
Secluded between was the architect's own private office.
Natural light for the room comes in through a skylight and a
window triptych that showers it with the colors of spring.
Wright had finally found his language for glass. Rectilinear lines
substituted for naturalistic shapes and told their own story.
Realism in glass was anathema to Wright; in 1928 he decried
anything that got "mixed up with the view outside" and
ordered that a "window pattern should stay severely put." He
had made a partnership with the machine. Squares, rectangles,
and bars weave themselves into a frame surrounding plain
plate glass. Privacy is protected without resorting to draperies
lacking "rhyme or sanitary reason," while the view is clearly
focused. Other Wright windows of the time used a similar
frame motif, including ones later removed from the studio
reception hall. Three years earlier Wright had lined his
children's playroom upstairs with glass screens whose square
motifs masqueraded as pale tulips, but here he took a step
forward into bold color. The windows are a reminder that the
delights of nature are never far away. Relatively simple glass
fills the rest of the studio and the entire house—Wright may
have saved some of the best glass for his own space.

THOMAS VESTIBULE

Mystery was at the heart of Wright's entrances. Visitors would often be required to snake along a circuitous path until finally the architect let them behold the door. To gain entry to the Thomas House in Oak Park, one travels under a ground-floor arch and up a flight of stairs, turns, ascends higher to the house's second floor—and steps into a glass-enclosed bower. Owners and visitors alike know that they have arrived. The extraordinary vestibule that Wright created here in 1901 reaches out to welcome like a clearing on the prairie. Recalling wispy prairie grass or plants, the doors and windows are dressed in squares and bars of opalescent glass and gold leaf topped by attenuated triangles. They screen the view, allowing light in but serving more subtly than any curtain to keep prying eyes out. Ceiling lights above elaborate on the feathery triangles; in the four corners mother-of-pearl applied to the glass heightens the golden effect. Tucked into the ell between the living and dining rooms, the entry is part of an almost unbroken band of glass, all fabricated by the glass designers Giannini and Hilgart, that makes the second-floor walls vanish. The roofs seem to float above. Wright had found a single tool with which to bring nature inside, naturally, and to break down solid walls. His great era of art glass had begun.

DANA WINDOWS

Susan Lawrence Dana's home in Springfield, Illinois, was a house of glass long before there were glass houses in America. Her wealth allowed Wright almost free rein in 1902 to create a wonderland where glass sparkled in hundreds of windows and doors, hanging lamps and standing lamps, sconces and skylights, as well as nooks and crannies in between. The glass display begins at the front door (right), where Wright took the old-fashioned idea of a fanlight and transformed it into a dancing brigade of butterflies *en pointe*. A pair of arches on either side of a glass vault reinforces the motif, which is unusual in the architect's more typical repertoire of stylized plant forms. Some say that the butterflies refer to an old fireplace left in the house, or to the house's roofline, or to the freedom of flight—or perhaps to Dana's role as a social butterfly. The greens, golds, and browns, in any case, bring inside the hues of a prairie autumn, when butterflies take wing. In the dining room and along the walkway to the gallery designed for entertaining, hanging lamps (pages 106–7) pick up the lepidopteran theme. Also in the dining room is an overscaled lunette presenting the house's signature sumac motif. A half-moon–shaped relative rises over the dramatic two-story gallery (pages 78–79), but it sings a different tune. The chevron shapes of sumac leaves and butterfly wings were forsaken in favor of rectilinear abstractions of plants. Side windows repeat its weave of squares and rectangles. Wright was said to be averse to unrelieved arches—perhaps they were too classical and symmetrical for him—so he bisected this lunette with horizontal and vertical wood trim. His associate Marion Mahony helped him design the acres of glass his office turned out during the Prairie years and no doubt assisted him with the Dana commission as she did for the Martin and Robie Houses and the Coonley Playhouse. Linden Glass Company of Chicago received the princely sum for the time of $15,000 to help turn Dana's house into an iridescent jewel.

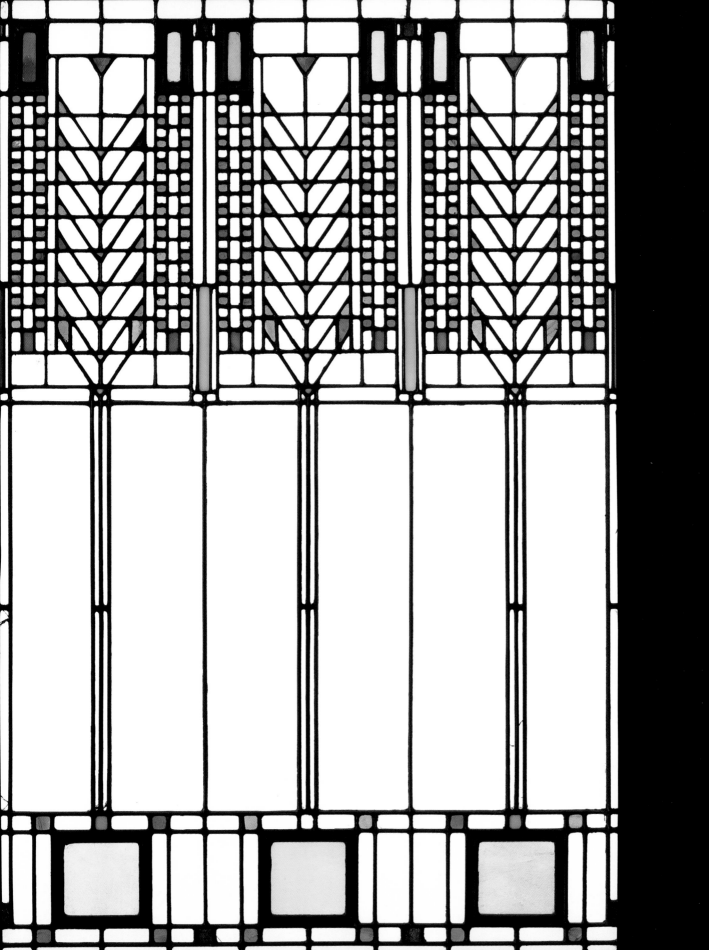

TREE OF LIFE WINDOW

Pattern, said Wright in 1928, "is made more cheaply and beautifully effective when introduced into the glass of the windows than in the use of any other medium that architecture has to offer." But he chose to use art glass not just for its patterns or even its colors. Thanks to a new electroglazing process designed to anchor the glass pieces, he was able to use metal tracery to add yet another layer of meaning to these screens of light. In few places is this concept as clear as in the windows of Darwin and Isabel Martin's house in Buffalo, New York, designed in 1904. Ringing the upper stories and lighting the reception hall, these windows have come to be known as the Tree of Life pattern because of their obvious debt to nature. Wright's desire to stylize plants and trees— inspiration without imitation—was entirely successful here. In this window, three geometric forms grow organically from square roots and branch out overhead in leaves formed from chevrons. The autumnal-colored glass, manufactured also by Linden Glass, sits in caming that etches the pattern in zinc and copper. As in many of Wright's windows, much of the glass is iridescent so that it takes on one hue in daylight and another at night. Clear glass fills the rest of each window for uninterrupted views. Used solo, in trios, and in quartets, the Tree of Life windows composed a sonata in glass for the Martins, a couple who enjoyed nature as much as Wright did.

MAY SKYLIGHT

For Wright, light did not stop at the ceiling. Early on in his
career as an architect and a glass designer, he moved his
windows up beyond the walls and turned them into skylights.
This elevated source sends light gently down into a room,
bathing it in a diffused glow. Wright created this effect both
with skylights that used the sun and with ceiling lights—he
called them "moonlight"—that relied on the new invention of
electricity. From window to high clerestory to skylight, a room
could be painted in well-balanced light. He combined all three
techniques in a nearly seamless composition for Sophie and
Meyer May's house in Grand Rapids, Michigan, completed in
1910. The living room faces south to coax in as much sunshine
as possible, helped along by a wall of geometrically patterned
art glass. Tall panels reach above the oak molding to a row of
clerestories. The banded square in the center, framed by
copper outside, repeats the square motif in the glass itself.
Like the molten material it once was, the glass slides up and
onto the ceiling, where coordinated skylights illuminate the
night or day. A glass-shaded lamp continues the theme, which
extends even to the feathery pattern on the embroidered table
runner; both were the work of George Mann Niedecken.
The wall has vanished and in its place is light. "Glass and light—
two forms of the same thing!" Wright exclaimed in 1928

MAY WINDOWS

Using the lines of the living room windows as his thread,
Wright wove a tapestry of glass throughout the May House.
A wall of windows in the dining room picks up its warp and
woof, and elements are echoed in a glass-front sideboard
and light standards attached to the table. The upstairs was not
forgotten. Even in one of the children's bedrooms, art glass
brings nature right indoors. The rows of golden squares top and
bottom were seen downstairs, but the central motif has been
changed and strengthened to suspend a leafy plant nearly in
the center of each window. Repeated in openings all along
the wall, it acts like a valence to increase the sense of privacy.
The parents' bedroom, a morning room for reading, and
another child's room open to the neighborhood with the
identical glass, which in intense sunlight casts magical patterns
on floors and ceilings. Now displayed in the corner child's
bedroom (in a house museum open to the public) is a set
of the Froebel blocks that set the young Wright himself on
his journey into architecture. They serve as a tactile reminder
of the geometry that was at the heart of all his designs.

COONLEY TRIPTYCH

Wright wrote music into the windows for the Coonley Playhouse of 1912 in Riverside, Illinois. He called them his "Kinder Symphony"—and what could be more appropriate for a school than these exuberant shapes and colors? For inspiration Wright turned not to nature but to that great American institution, the parade. Balloons fly high in the air, tangling on occasion with square confetti. A flag waves in the breeze. Variations on this central triptych lined the side walls in bands of clerestories raised well above the heads of the young children. Compared to the subdued natural tones used in his earlier glass, the primary colors are almost shockingly daring. Wright thought that their "primitive color" caused less interference with a window's function and added "a higher architectural note to the effect of *light* itself." Some credit for his change in palette and form may go to Wright's stay in Europe during 1909 and 1910, when he was probably exposed to the newly emerging abstract art. If so, he transformed those ideas into a medium of which he was the master: glass was Wright's best canvas. He had long had a fascination with balloons, bringing them home to his children to float in their tall playroom with its bursting ceiling. "Human beings," observed Wright in 1932, "are really childlike, in the best sense, when directly appealed to by simple, strong forms and pure, bright color." These curvilinear forms never left him; he pulled them out again the next year at Midway Gardens and continued to roll them around in one material or another—think of the Guggenheim Museum of Art—until the end of his career.

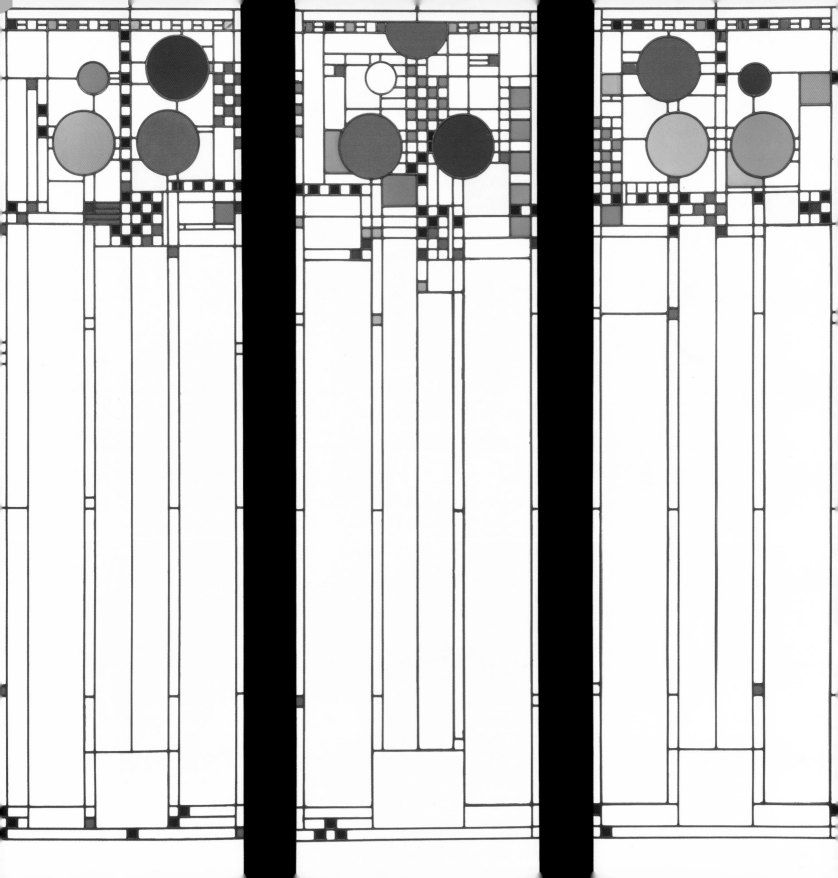

TALIESIN WINDOW

Wright thought of Taliesin, his home in Spring Green, Wisconsin, as "a broad shelter seeking fellowship with its surroundings." It was his "shining brow" (its meaning in Welsh), built not *on* the hill but *of* it. The architect spent boyhood summers in his family's gently rolling river landscape and returned in 1911 to fit a new home for himself into its beloved hills. It was to be a natural house in every sense, and Wright opened it to nature from nearly every room. Fires tragically destroyed the living quarters not just once, in 1914, but again in 1925. Taliesin rose a third time afterward—Wright's own phoenix, his work in progress over the three and a half decades remaining to him. The living room offers one of the most engaging views, focused through an art glass window from the Heath House of 1905 in Buffalo, New York. An architectural scavenger of sorts, Wright was adept at acquiring clients' castoffs or adapting previous designs for use in his own homes (the barrel chairs in the nearby dining alcove, for one). The Prairie-style window's feathery geometry of squares, diamonds, triangles, and parallelograms suits its new home, particularly when it mirrors the valley's fall colors. Glass meets the layered wall of limestone, a reminder of the riverbed below, without need of any distracting sash or frame. A sweeping "birdwalk," added in 1953, thrusts itself right into nature, where just like Wright's glass the lakes "catch . . . the sky."

HOLLYHOCK WINDOWS

In 1917, as Aline Barnsdall and Wright were in the throes of
"birth pangs," as Wright characterized their efforts to build her
a theater and house in Hollywood, Barnsdall herself gave birth.
The theatrical oil heiress was not married. Moving her little
Sugar Top (Aline Elizabeth, later known as Betty) into a home
became a priority. Any child, not to mention her mother,
should have been delighted with the suite that Wright finally
designed. Hollyhock House's child's quarters on the first floor
numbered a bedroom, a dressing room, a bathroom, space
for a nursemaid, and this playroom where art glass patterns
danced in a magical kingdom for one. (Overhead was the
room intended for Mother Barnsdall, who decided to sleep
downstairs.) In this house built around open courtyards, well
out of the California sun's glare, glass was a vital component.
The playroom's side walls, each filled with four panels of glass,
mysteriously slope inward five degrees. The ceiling is low, as
Wright liked it, creating just the right childlike scale here.
Bordered by sidelights mitered at the corners, the glassy door
at the far end releases the tension and opens up the space.
Triangles on the diagonal dart in from the sides and down from
the tops of the panels, carrying out the glass theme introduced
in the house's living spaces. More abstract even than most
of Wright's earlier glass designs, the door is symmetrical
while the sides explore abstraction's unlimited possibilities.
The door pattern reaches toward the ceiling as hollyhocks
push skyward. Purple, an unusual color in Wright's palette, may
have been suggested by Sugar Top's mother, who pointed it
out in some of her architect's Japanese prints. Judson Studio,
a noted art glass maker in Los Angeles, fabricated the windows. The young émigré architect Rudolph M. Schindler
helped supervise construction of the house and later explained
its windows: "They are not wall holes but a dissolution of the
building material into a grid—leaded glass—as the ground
dissolves and becomes lost in the tree branches." His astute
observation describes all of Wright's forays into art glass.

ENNIS WINDOW

The art glass in Hollyhock House had its roots in the architect's Prairie years, but three of the other four Los Angeles–area houses he designed in the early 1920s, all built of innovative concrete blocks, went without such windows. The textile patterns woven by the blocks themselves produced nearly all the ornament these progressive houses needed. That art glass reappeared in Wright's 1923 house for Mabel and Charles Ennis, the last of the textile-block houses, remains somewhat of a puzzle. It is certainly one of the last of Wright's houses to have art glass, and it may have been dictated by the owners, who made a number of changes at odds with the building's conception. Hardly anyone, however, could wish away the view of Los Angeles framed by the towering dining room window. Its three-part composition, almost classically Palladian, resonates with delicate tracery. The same diagonals used in the Hollyhock windows appear here, but the stark abstraction paints a flatness not seen in Wright's early work. Other glass in the house, such as the library doors, drips with lush hanging vines in complex combinations more reminiscent of his early midwestern commissions. If they are meant to be wisteria—portrayed more realistically in a glass fireplace mosaic in the loggia—fingers may point to Orlando Giannini. An artist responsible for murals in Wright's Oak Park home, Giannini had also executed similar wisteria overmantels for the houses of the Hussers (1899) in Chicago and the Darwin Martins (1904) in Buffalo, New York, both now lost. Some of the Ennis windows branch out into feather and arrow motifs—an interest in American Indians that Giannini shared with Wright.

PYREX GLASS TUBING

By the time Wright came to design an office building for the maker of Johnson Wax in 1936, flat planes were giving way to curves in his work. In the Administration Building, the first of two workspaces built for the S. C. Johnson Company's headquarters in Racine, Wisconsin, the circle holds sway: in the tops of the dendriform columns in the Great Workroom, in the sinuous curves of the desks, in the narrow red piping around the chairs (pages 48–49). The glass followed suit. At first, to push light into the far reaches, Wright had in mind to use prism glass like his Luxfer designs of four decades earlier. Because the building turns away from its setting, drawing light inside was a major hurdle for the architect. He soon tossed out his nineteenth-century material and settled on a unique solution after envisioning the possibilities that lay in modern technology. When the Corning Glass Company said that it could make Pyrex glass tubes a mile long if he wanted, Wright was off and running with this new tool. The translucent tubing not only would bring in light without distraction, its sealed air was also its own insulation. He stretched it into a canopy of light, ringed the cornice line with it, snipped it into geometric patterns on walls, and molded a dome filled with encircling constellations. Rhythmic patterns arose from the necessary act of joining the tubes. More weatherproof adhesives since invented have replaced the originals. Today light still softly filters over the Johnson Wax employees from Wright's inspiration of long ago. When day turns to night, light bulbs take the sun's place in this universe of one man's creation.

95

DECORAT

Details mattered to Wright, and none were too small to escape his notice.

An urn to hold dried flowers from the prairie. A lamp for a library table.

China for all occasions. Carpets and upholstery fabrics to signify the mod-

ern age and classical sculpture to remember civilizations long past. Fireplace

accoutrements—and even the mortar in the wall itself. Each decorative

IVE ARTS

object chosen for a Wright house was carefully integrated into the overall scheme. Geometric designs in art glass were matched in the lamp shades. Patterns in a rug were echoed in embroidered table linens and runners. Wright's respect for Japanese simplicity is obvious in the design and placement of these items: each stroke is vital to his picture of domestic serenity.

WINGED VICTORY

Even Frank Lloyd Wright did not dare to claim that he created the Winged Victory (*Nike of Samothrace*). But plaster casts of this world-famous Hellenistic sculpture from the second century B.C. found their way into the houses of many of his early clients as well as his home in Oak Park. Before he gained the confidence to design his own decorative objects, Wright liked to add a touch of antiquity as "worthy entertainment" for the eye. Once he traveled to Japan in 1905, he intensified his efforts to collect all things Japanese: prints in particular but also pottery, sculpture, screens, and other antiques. At Taliesin, his home in Wisconsin after 1911, he gave them prized places, where they stood as "messengers … from other civilizations." Historic objects were spirits of peace and good will, traces of the human spirit "left behind in the human procession as Time went on," Wright wrote in his 1932 *Autobiography*. As "ancient comment on the New," they heightened the stark contrast between the old order and the new one he was inventing. For those who did not have rare oriental objects, reproductions of the *Nike* would do. His clients the Littles are known to have displayed a copy in the living room of their second Wright home in Wayzata, Minnesota (right), designed in 1912, and he placed one over the doorway in his children's playroom in Oak Park (page 100). Another guarded the atrium of the Larkin Administration Building of 1903 in Buffalo, New York, and still others were sketched into Wright's presentation drawings for various clients. Ward and Cecilia Willits of Highland Park, Illinois, accompanied Frank and Catherine Wright to Japan in 1905, where they may have acquired some relics of their own, but today it is the iconic Greek statue that guards the top of the stair hall in their 1902 Wright house (page 101). In Wright's day the Winged Victory was a powerful symbol of flight—landed on the prow of a ship, the goddess embodied motion itself. With her wings spread tautly behind her, she still seems to be flying. Her wet garments both cling and swirl, allowing for the play of light and dark. A votive figure, this monument to victory originally graced a shrine, as perhaps Wright may have visualized her in his own architecture.

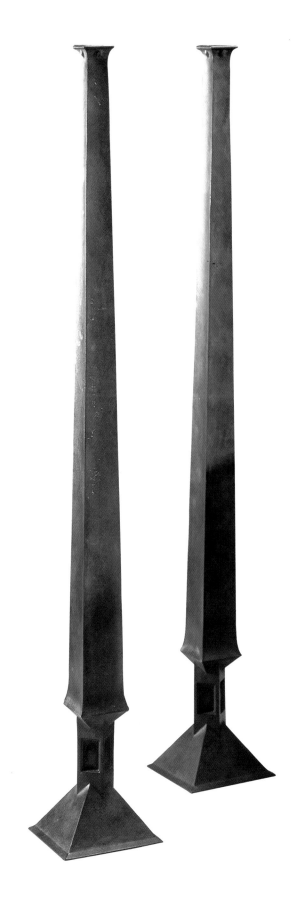

COPPER VASES

Wright was intrigued by relics from ancient civilizations, but it did not take him long to realize that his own creativity might be a match for the talents of the artists of Greece, China, and Japan. Conjuring up artistic objects for a home, he recalled in his 1932 *Autobiography*, was "the most fascinating phase of the work, involving the true poetry of conception." He began working with decorative arts at the apogee of the Arts and Crafts movement, whose practitioners were exploring new forms that expressed the harmony of nature. Like a number of these designers, Wright turned to metalwork and "fell in love with sheet copper as a building material." Two extraordinary vases—one a tall, attenuated weed holder, the other a squat, rotund urn—were made and parceled out to select clients beginning about 1895–98. The urn, shaped from répousée, not cast, copper, is a study in circles and squares (opposite). Rising from a crossed base, its four circular motifs mirror the object's own round form but are reined in by squares and intersecting geometric motifs. Standing on a pyramidal base, the weed holder, in contrast, is the essence of simplicity— proud testimony to the ability of the machine (left). Its sleek form seems to forecast the mile-high skyscraper Wright proposed for Chicago in 1954. Both vases were made by James A. Miller and Brother of Chicago, a firm Wright knew from his early days working for Adler and Sullivan. And both appear in drawings and photographs of the period: in Wright's Oak Park home and studio; at the Waller (1899), Dana (1902), and Coonley (1907) Houses in Illinois; at the long-gone Browne's Bookstore (1907) in Chicago; and at an architectural exhibit of the architect's favorite work in 1902. Wright wanted each urn and vase filled with summer blossoms, dried flowers, or even weeds—anything that would be a reminder of nature's fields and woods. Copper's autumnal tones made it the perfect vessel for these plants and Wright's houses. He later produced silver services for the Imperial Hotel (1915–23) in Tokyo, but it was copper that captured his true colors.

PEDESTAL LAMP

Electric lights had barely come on the scene—perfected during his boyhood in the 1880s—when Wright began his work as an architect. It was a novel toy for a designer who remained challenged by new technology all his life. As with everything else, he integrated it into the fabric of each site. "No longer an appliance nor even an appurtenance," said Wright in 1928 about his early lighting, "but really architecture ... made a part of the building." For Susan Lawrence Dana's 1902 home in Springfield, Illinois, he made the house itself shine like a glass prism. Thousands of facets reflected light from art glass windows and doors, skylights and sconces, and ingenious table lamps resembling Wright's buildings. His double-pedestal lamp for the Dana House is rightly famous. Hovering above

sturdy bronze-and-glass piers, the hipped shade calls to mind a sheltering Prairie-style roof. The leaded glass pattern repeats the stylized sumac refrain and prairie hues that turn the grand house into an autumn forest. Cube feet provide a solid foundation. Not to be outdone, a related single-pedestal lamp in the house fans out into a sixteen-sided glass shade—an umbrella of soft, colored light. Wright placed similar but less impressive lamps in other Prairie houses, such as the Heath House (1905) in Buffalo, New York, and the Robie House (1908) in Chicago. The spindled oak armchair, a variant of his tall-back dining chairs, appeared in different forms in other houses of the period. Paired with the double-pedestal lamp in the library, it created a cozy reading nook inviting one to linger.

BUTTERFLY LAMP

In 1902, the year in which Wright began designing the Dana House in Springfield, Illinois, he announced that he considered "everything in the nature of a hanging fixture a weakness." What he had in mind in those early days of electricity was the bare bulb that jangled lonely from the ceiling at the tail end of a naked cord. His solution here was a delicate butterfly whose wings metamorphosed into shimmering glass. Four chandeliers in the dining room and another hanging lamp in the stair landing near the gallery are part of the same swarm that greets visitors in the glass transom over the front door (pages 76–77). In the dining room these lemony butterflies seem poised to feast on the goldenrod and purple aster in the mural ringing the walls. Fabricated by the Linden Glass Company of Chicago, the composition reinforces the sumac motif of the house's glass and lamps but is an unusually complex interweaving of planes. In the stair landing that serves as a platform to the gallery, the lamp's modernity is a foil for another of Wright's favorite antiquities, the Venus of Milo (*Aphrodite of Melos*). He may have liked the way the rough folds of her drapery set off her smooth skin, or how light plays against shadow—contrasts that appear in his own work. Sculpted in the late second century B.C. but not rediscovered until 1820, this Hellenistic ideal of beauty remained compelling to Wright in the early years of his independent practice. A nearly life-size version kept watch over the drafting tables in his Oak Park studio, no doubt offering inspiration, and he prescribed Venus for clients along with the Winged Victory (pages 98–101). Here in the Dana House, surrounded by Wright's new masterpieces, she stands as if preserved in a glass vitrine.

"FLOWER" SCULPTURE

A modern-day Venus awaits visitors as they enter Susan Lawrence Dana's house in Springfield, Illinois. At first sight this terra-cotta sculpture seems a world apart from the classic *Aphrodite* at the far end of the house. Realism has given way—in part—to abstraction; sensuous curves have yielded—in part—to geometric forms. But the arms and face of the *Flower in the Crannied Wall* retain the gentle classical beauty of her forebears. She is a provocative enigma. Wright conceived the idea for the sculpture, based on a Tennyson poem of the same name, but it was executed by Richard Bock in 1904 after a previous sculptor failed to translate Wright's vision into stone. The nude figure—nature? the architectural muse?—rises from the same block as a geometric, skyscraper-stepped pylon, nurturing a structure as organic as one of Wright's buildings. Inscribed on the back of the sculpture are Tennyson's lines, which Wright had liked enough to include in *The House Beautiful,* the book he designed in 1896:

> Flower in the crannied wall,
> I pluck you out of the crannies,
> I hold you here, root and all, in my hand,
> Little flower—but if I could understand
> What you are, root and all, and all in all,
> I should know what God and man is.

In the living hall directly behind, a fire screen and a tall, octagonal Teco vase repeat the statue's Wrightian motifs. But it took the architect another decade to relinquish the last vestiges of classicism in his sculpture. At Midway Gardens in Chicago in 1913, working this time with Alfonso Iannelli, he pared a host of sculpted concrete sprites to their geometric essence. The *Flower in the Crannied Wall,* however, remains the purest expression of the roots of Wright's own creativity.

GOLDEN MORTAR

Families gathered around the warming hearth—this was
the picture of domestic tranquillity Wright liked to paint
in his houses. From Chicago to South Carolina to southern
California, each of his homes had a fireplace, if not several.
The hearth was the dominant furnishing in every Wright
house. Solidly built into the core of the structure itself, it
was as integral as any ornament could be: arched with brick,
framed by a slab lintel, or opening from a cave of stones.
Of all his fireplace designs, one stands out for its ingenuity
and audacity. For the May House in Grand Rapids, Michigan,
completed in 1910, Wright faced the mortar with slices of
iridescent glass. A brick and limestone fireplace in the living
room fills the wall opposite a south-facing bank of windows.
When the sun streams in, the glass turns to golden light, the
mortar vanishes, and the bricks seem suspended weightlessly
in air. Turned to mirrors, the glass reflects the autumnal colors
of the house. It was a sleight of hand only a magician such as
Wright could carry off impeccably. A smaller version of the
fireplace illuminates the master bedroom upstairs. Just as
Wright worked to destroy the confining walls of houses, here
he dematerialized once-solid bricks and mortar. He suffused
this home with light from an unexpected source and created
a reminder of the very flat plane of the prairie outside.

IMPERIAL CHINA

The Imperial Hotel in Tokyo, built between 1915 and 1923, was Wright's *magnum opus*. Inside its solid stone walls was a symphonic blend of custom furniture, carpets, textiles, lamps, silver services for tea and coffee, and china to fill three different dining needs. Just a few years earlier, for Chicago's vibrant Midway Gardens, Wright had designed his first dinnerware. For that he chose to ring oval white dishes with a pattern resembling square confetti—his son John Lloyd Wright called them "vermilion beauty spots." When Wright reached Tokyo, it seems that Midway was still on his mind. He picked up the circles that had enlivened several murals there, as well as the windows in the Coonley Playhouse (page 87), and scattered them on the dinner service for the hotel's cabaret dining room. The overlapping disks in red, yellow, green, and blue are poignant reminders of Wright's failed hopes for Midway, which was left unfinished and then went bankrupt in 1916, falling to the wreckers in 1929.

Festive circles float like champagne bubbles over the sides of some of the seven pieces and down into the porcelain bowls. One circle encloses the Imperial's "IH" monogram. Beginning about 1922, several versions of this design were created and used in the hotel. For its more formal dining room, Wright designed an elegant gold-ringed pattern of crosses built of squares; a short pendant motif recalled the building's architecture and was repeated on a third and simpler set of room-service china. Even before the hotel was demolished in 1968, reproductions of the lively cabaret china by Noritake allowed admirers to set their own dinner tables with it. At the Lovness House of 1955 in Stillwater, Minnesota, the dashing circles make perfect counterpoints for the square cushions covered in Wright's favorite red. The pattern actually seems more at home here—as it would have been at Midway—than in the exotic halls of the Imperial Hotel. It was an idea that may have come too late for Midway, but Wright was not yet done with it.

112

TALIESIN LAMP

Among the first lighting fixtures Wright designed was a lacy fretwork screen of wood recessed into the ceiling above his Oak Park dining table. The house had been electrified just four years before Wright redesigned the dining space in 1895, but he was quick to devise a novel way to install electric light behind a thin membrane of rice paper. Filtered through this screen of wood and paper, beams embraced the Wright family "as sunlight sifts through leaves in the trees," he said. Even larger panels lighted the children's playroom on the second floor. Three decades later, in 1925, Wright reassembled these early materials into a table lamp that has become one of his most recognized furnishings. Used first at Taliesin, his Wisconsin home, the lamp turns three squares into a source of softly diffused light. At the top a small square opening makes room for the socket and lets air circulate, while the shade slopes downward into a larger square, which is itself mirrored in a square wooden base. Hipped like Wright's Prairie-style roofs, the shade hangs from a cantilevered arm to completely shelter the bulb. Tapered ribs mark its sides. Envious clients asked Wright for similar versions for their own homes, and he complied at times with identical lamps and at others with shades that substituted cloth for rice paper. Wright had experimented ten years earlier with lamps cantilevered over the dining tables of Midway Gardens in Chicago. As he worked on the Imperial Hotel in Tokyo into the 1920s, the idea no doubt benefited from the Japanese aesthetic. Back home at Taliesin, he used the new lamp to keep a subtle reminder of Japan with him as he read in his bedroom-study.

GLASS·LESS LIGHT

Always perfecting designs that he especially liked, Wright
again returned to his past in 1932 for another lamp. In 1914
he had developed a standing light fixture for the Summer
Garden terrace of Midway Gardens, his European-style entertainment center in Chicago. Placed alongside tall, geometric
spires by Alfonso Iannelli, Wright's lamps stepped eleven cubes
of light upward on either side of a pole—staggered lights that
made a stairway to the stars. Nearly two decades later, when
he needed hanging fixtures for the Hillside Playhouse at Taliesin, Wright plucked the Midway design from his repertoire
but transformed it into wood. To light the space without glass,
he placed bulbs into open wooden boxes angled in opposite
directions around a wooden pole. Flat, rectangular reflectors
softly directed the light downward from these "magically
hanging pendants." This lamp also had great appeal to Wright
clients, for whom he created various versions that stood
on the floor or a table or were built into the wall (pages 51
and 113). In these, the light boxes were turned to 90- or
180-degree angles and the reflecting shades were above or
below, depending on the light needed. Unlighted, the lamp
is pure Wrightian sculpture. Lighted, it bathes a house in the
mysteriousness that Wright worked so diligently to produce.

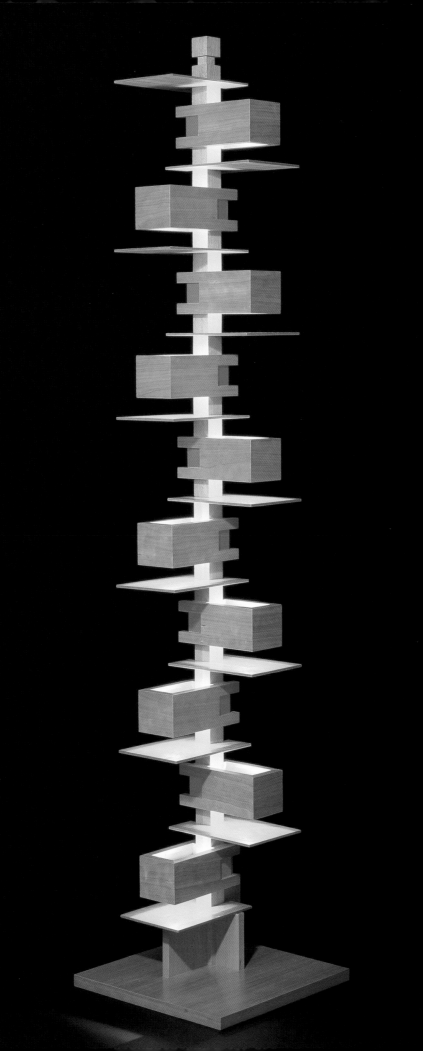

FIREPLACE KETTLE

Wright not only gave each house a fireplace, he often designed the equipment for it. Fire screens, andirons, and grates completed this composition at the heart of the home. Nestled into its rocky promontory above Bear Run in Pennsylvania, Fallingwater demanded a hearth as spectacular as its setting. In 1935 Wright shaped Edgar and Lilianne Kaufmann's fireplace out of local sandstone, situating it carefully behind a boulder found on the site and simply left in place. That was all he needed for a hearth. But Wright did not stop with an iron grate in the same red used for accent throughout the house. He devised a spherical kettle suspended from an arm holding an intricate system of hooks and supports. When not in use, the kettle was to be swung back into a specially carved niche in the wall. On cold evenings, when some hot mulled wine or cider was called for, it was meant to be shifted over the center of the fire. By his implements, Wright helped define the lifestyles of his clients. The kettle's circular shape—a red balloon from the Coonley Playhouse windows turned to metal—was one that the architect found increasingly fascinating in his later years. The kettle itself reappeared in other Wright commissions, first at Wingspread, the house he designed for the Johnson family near Racine, Wisconsin, in 1937. There, the three-story freestanding fireplace is itself rounded as if to accommodate the kettle. But in others—such as the Neils House (1949) in Minneapolis and the Usonian Exhibition House (1953) in New York—the round kettles, usually black, contrast strikingly with the rectilinear fireplaces, as if they were a punctuation mark left as part of Wright's signature.

WOOD SCREENS

Screens were among Wright's earliest devices for subtly
dividing spaces and diffusing light. At his Oak Park home he
placed them overhead in 1895 as sawn-wood light fixtures.
In his Prairie-style houses during the early 1900s he spindled
them to interrupt a view without closing it off, to reveal but
not conceal. And by the time he entered his Usonian phase in
the mid- to late 1930s, he had determined that screens could
replace most other ornament and stand alone as a house's
defining decorative feature. For these efficient homes of
modest cost, Wright created wood cutouts that screened
windows and clerestories as well as features in the open
interiors. The complex art glass of his earlier houses was too
expensive for these Usonians, but their owners could make
do just fine with geometric wood panels that channeled views
in much the same way. Some of the richest paneling of this
type can be found in the home that Sara and Melvyn Maxwell
Smith built over four years in Bloomfield Hills, Michigan,
beginning in 1946. A stepped motif cut from Tidewater
cypress faces doors to the terrace and, above the dining table,
draws "moonlight" into the compact space at the elbow of the
L-shaped plan. In a small sitting area, a folding screen sets apart
the inner sanctum. Like trees growing in a forest, the cutouts
bring nature indoors. Warm wood such as this, said Wright,
is lovely to the touch and "grateful to the eye." As ornament,
it is organically woven into the fabric of the house itself.

PATTERNED CARPET

What was underfoot was as important to Wright as the ceiling, the walls, and all the furnishings in between. Despite this, he was rarely allowed to finish his buildings with carpets that pulled together all their design elements. Of his outstanding examples—such as those for the Coonley (1907), Robie (1908), May (1908), and Bogk (1916) Houses during his Prairie years and the Imperial Hotel in the early 1920s—the carpet designed in 1951 for his son David Wright shows how active the architect's imagination remained even at the age of eighty-four. Built in the desert of Phoenix, Arizona, in the midst of a citrus orchard, the house (based on a plan called "How to Live in the Southwest") spirals up from a ground-floor garden court to a ring of living quarters on the upper level. It is a swirl of concrete block, and Wright gave his son and daughter-in-law, Gladys, a swirling confection of a carpet to reinforce its spherical shape. Balloons of many colors and sizes bounce off one another in a tightly controlled nod to whimsy. In 1926–27 Wright had designed a similar pattern as one of twelve monthly covers for *Liberty* magazine; they were rejected then as too exuberant, but, transferred to vibrant yarn, the March design at last found a good home. The *Liberty* designs, Wright once explained, were for "the Children, obvious arrangements of familiar objects or easy abstractions—intended to be 'not too difficult.'" His play with spheres can be traced back to the Coonley Playhouse windows of 1912 (page 87) and two murals executed for Midway Gardens in 1913. Whatever the medium, he clearly found delight in what his compass had to offer. The wide range of colors in this carpet found its counterpart four years later with the release of Wright's Taliesin Palette of paint colors for the Martin-Senour Company. And in 1957 Wright tried his hand at another carpet filled with interlocking circles but was rebuffed when his client Maximilian Hoffman said no to Wright's vision for his house in Rye, New York. In 1959, however, after the architect's death, the carpet maker V'Soske (manufacturer also of the David Wright carpet) loomed the Hoffman design and it was placed in the living-dining area at Taliesin in Wisconsin.

FABRIC NO. 105

Wright never had complete success with his carpets—even a commercial line planned for release by Karastan in 1956 never made it off the drafting boards. Better luck came with mass-produced fabrics and wallpapers offered by F. Schumacher and Company beginning in 1955. For sixty years before this, Wright had insisted that each of his designs was unique: a response individually fitted to the needs at hand. And wallpaper had been a tool of "inferior desecrators," not of Wright. But in the 1950s he was persuaded, in large part by Elizabeth Gordon, the editor of *House Beautiful,* to lend his name to furniture, paint, textiles, and wall coverings that middle-class buyers could purchase for their own homes. If they could not come to Wright directly for a house, he could come to them in care-fully conceived patterns and colors designed to harmonize with a range of living places. Schumacher and Wright worked together to create some designs that were adapted by the company from Wright's work and others that the Taliesin Fellowship designed based on items such as architectural plans (see the book's endpapers). Design No. 105, offered as both linen and wallpaper, was inspired by a carpet in Wright's Coonley House of 1907 in Riverside, Illinois, one of his great Prairie houses. In its translation to a different time and use., the strongly rectilinear design showed its longevity and its universality. Wright himself proved his flexibility, his ability to change with the times. Over the years Schumacher has introduced other lines of Wright furnishings, even rugs, underscoring the staying power of Wright's vision and his concern that not one single item—not the furniture, not the windows, not the small objects that bring joy to daily life—should be overlooked in furnishing a house to make it a home.

124

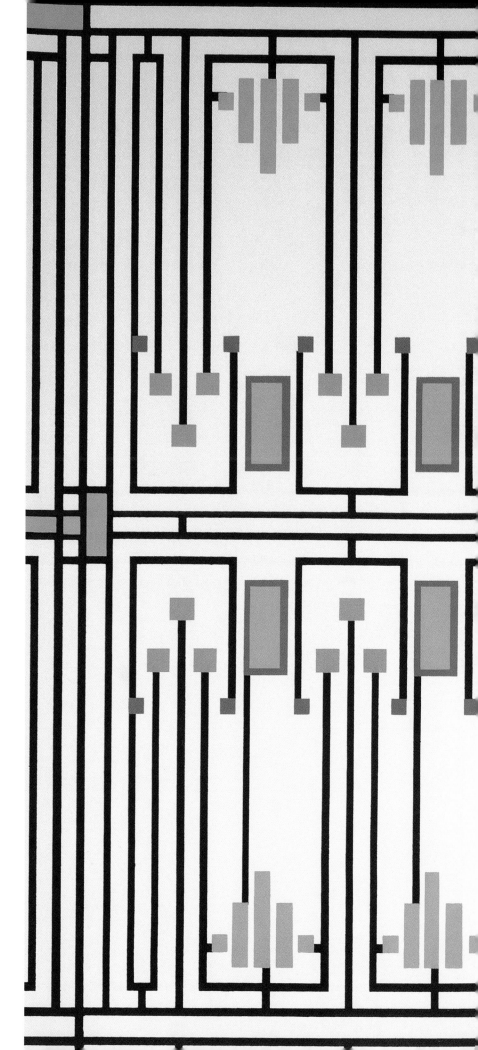

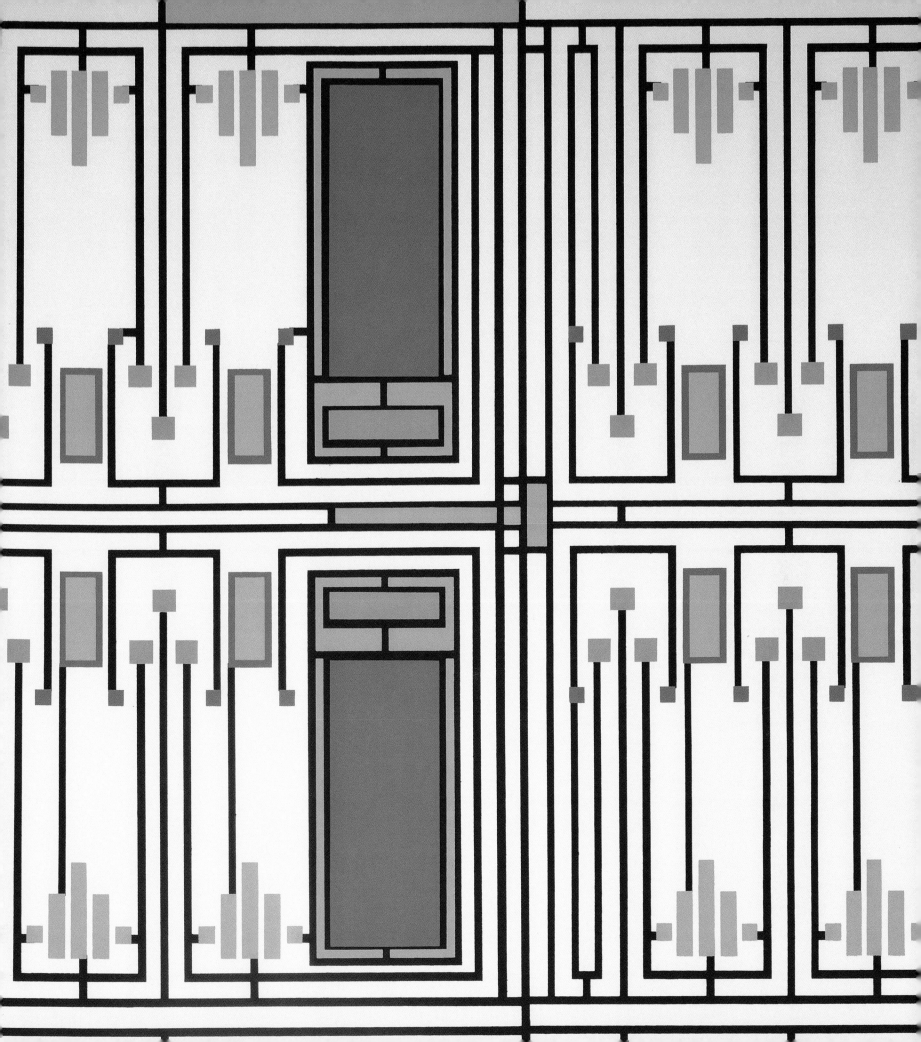

SELECTED BIBLIOGRAPHY

Fowler, Penny. "Please Be Crated." In *Frank Lloyd Wright: The Seat of Genius. Chairs: 1895–1955.* West Palm Beach, Fla.: Eaton Fine Art, 1997.

Frank Lloyd Wright Quarterly, 1990–99.

Hanks, David A. *The Decorative Designs of Frank Lloyd Wright.* New York: Dutton, 1979.

———. *Frank Lloyd Wright: Preserving an Architectural Heritage. Decorative Designs from The Domino's Pizza Collection.* New York: Dutton, 1989.

Harrington, Elaine. *Frank Lloyd Wright Home and Studio, Oak Park.* Stuttgart: Edition Axel Menges, 1996.

Heinz, Thomas A. *Frank Lloyd Wright: Glass Art.* London: Academy Editions, 1994.

———. *Frank Lloyd Wright: Interiors and Furniture.* London: Academy Editions, 1994.

Hoffmann, Donald. *Frank Lloyd Wright's Dana House.* New York: Dover, 1996.

———. *Frank Lloyd Wright's Hollyhock House.* New York: Dover, 1992.

Kaufmann, Edgar, Jr. *Frank Lloyd Wright at the Metropolitan Museum of Art.* New York: Metropolitan Museum of Art, 1985.

Lind, Carla. *Lost Wright: Frank Lloyd Wright's Vanished Masterpieces.* New York: Simon and Schuster, 1996.

———. *Wright at a Glance Series.* 12 vols. San Francisco: Pomegranate, 1994–96.

———. *The Wright Style.* New York: Simon and Schuster, 1992.

Pfeiffer, Bruce Brooks. *Frank Lloyd Wright: The Masterworks.* New York: Rizzoli, 1993.

Robertson, Cheryl. *Frank Lloyd Wright and George Mann Niedecken: Prairie School Collaborators.* Lexington, Mass.: Milwaukee Art Museum and Museum of Our National Heritage, 1999.

Secrest, Meryle. *Frank Lloyd Wright.* New York: Knopf, 1992.

Sittenfeld, Michael, ed. *The Prairie School: Design Vision for the Midwest.* The Art Institute of Chicago Museum Studies, vol. 21, no. 2, 1995.

Storrer, William Allin. *The Frank Lloyd Wright Companion.* Chicago: University of Chicago Press, 1993.

Wright, Frank Lloyd. *Frank Lloyd Wright: Collected Writings.* 5 vols. Edited by Bruce Brooks Pfeiffer. New York: Rizzoli, 1992–95.

PHOTOGRAPH CREDITS

INDEX